DON'T
WEEP
for ME

DON'T WEEP for ME

by
claudette e. sims

An IMPRESSIONS Book

DON'T WEEP FOR ME

ISBN: 0-9616121-0-X
Library of Congress Catalog Book Number 85-82124

Cover graphics by Mauri Williams

Published by
IMPRESSIONS
P.O.Box 270502
Houston, Texas 77277
(713) 995-4440

Printed in the United States of America

". . . we will either find a way or make one"

This book is dedicated
to my Aunt Gladys
who departed this life
on December 26, 1978
and to my mother, Evangeline,
who is a living, breathing example
of the strength, courage and endurance
of women everywhere.

FOREWORD

There are an estimated 30 million single women in the United States for 21.5 million single men.*

Simply stated . . . something ain't right!

* Source: U.S. Census Bureau (1989)

CONTENTS

"Little girls grow up dreaming of ways to catch a man.
Little boys grow up dreaming of ways to buy a car.
Therein lies the problem."

Don't Weep For Me is not an autobiography. If by some miracle, I had managed to survive all of the nerds, turds, jerks, weirdos and crazies described in the following pages, I would not be *writing* a book . . . I'd be curled up in a straightjacket *eating* a book!

claudette e. sims

". . . the busy have no time for tears"

CHAPTER **1**

A PEP TALK

First and foremost, let's get something straight right off the top. Being single is not an illness or a disease. It is not contagious or inflammatory. It is not a condition. It is a state and the word "single" simply means not married . . . period.

Being single means sometimes being alone but being alone doesn't necessarily mean loneliness. In fact, there is seldom a good excuse for being lonely. We have all been given an invitation to life (we're breathing, aren't we?) and if you choose to spend three quarters of your life waiting for someone else to make you happy, to fulfill your dreams and share your space, you deserve to be lonely!

This book will explain why you are the conductor of your life and the pilot of your plane (regardless of who comes along for the ride). It will also show you how

1

important it is to believe in yourself and in your dreams, always realizing that love and happiness is around the next corner if you take charge of your life. You've already made the first step by buying this book (God bless you) so onward and upward!

"... a woman who waits for a knight in shining armor to sweep her off her feet usually ends up cleaning up after his horse"

CHAPTER 2

THE PROBLEM

As little girls growing up, very few of us really ever seriously thought that we would have to walk through life alone, without a mate . . . someone to love and take care of us and "make us feel complete."

But today, there are an estimated 30 million single women in the United States and only 21.5 million single men. Subtract the undesirables (we'll discuss them later) and the number of available men becomes even smaller. Multiply the problem by the ever-present burden of color and the history of sexism, racism and oppression in America, and the number of desirable single Black men dwindles even further.

The truth of the matter is that there is a crisis in Black America—a crisis that is not exclusive to Black America but one that is magnified in Black communities across the

3

nation. Why? Because when America catches a cold, Black America gets the flu. When America gets hypertension, Black America has a stroke.

Don't Weep For Me is a survival guide for single women who have finally decided that they alone are responsible for their happiness. It is for women who are 25 or 35 or 55 who believe they have a right to a fulfilling life and understand that only they can make the decision to have one.

This book is based on my belief that life is worth living without a man! Case closed! Sure, you can sit at home and do your nails five nights a week or crochet Christmas gifts in April. Or you can go to bed each night dreaming of Prince Charming and that stupid white horse. And you can certainly lead a dull life if you want to.

But just because you're single doesn't mean you're powerless to do anything to improve the quality of your life. You don't have to be a victim of circumstances. If you don't like your life, change it. Start with finding out who you are and what you want. Learn to chase away the blues, dispose of the emotional baggage and get on with your life. Tell loneliness, depression, anxiety and fear to go to hell! How can you see your happiness if your eyes are always clouded with tears and your heart is overflowing with self-pity?

Make a promise to yourself today to stop crying yourself into a coma every Saturday night and go for it!

"... wisdom is immortal"

CHAPTER **3**

THE GREAT
AMERICAN TRAGEDY

For centuries, marriage has been regarded as an American institution, a tradition never to be broken. But the ugly statistics of the 80s and 90s—where men and women are making the difficult decision to end fifteen or twenty year marriages in search of happiness, fulfillment and contentment—are a reality. It is also a testimony to the fact that in the life process—from birth to death—marriage is just a stage. Sometimes a temporary stage, sometimes more permanent than temporary, but nevertheless, a stage like starting first grade, adjusting to a new job or a new pair of shoes.

Black women must be deprogrammed on the subject of marriage. We must learn to see marriage as a pleasant but not necessary stage in our growth. If we are to survive the crisis facing us today, we must learn to criticize the system that has historically forced us into "singles court." The charge? "You mean you're 25 years old and not married yet?" We must question our own real and imagined fears about living our lives without a man. We must realistically explore our options and if we choose (and we must) to live each day to the fullest, our newfound attitudes will have a chilling effect on the attitudes and behavior of our men and society-at-large.

One of the major accomplishments of the civil rights movement—in addition to the right vote, riding in the front of the bus and eating in restaurants—was our right to make a choice. The choice to be or not to be, to screw or not to screw, to do or die. With the gift of free choice, however, has come major responsibilities. You can become a slave to love or let love become a slave to you. You can take responsibility for your own hurt or get hurt over and over and over again.

It's not entirely our fault however. The truth is that fairy tales did not prepare us for the roles we're playing. We grew up as many little girls did—black and white—in the late 40s and mid 50s—reading about Cinderella (I still don't believe she was hooked on a guy with a shoe fetish) and hearing about Snow White and the Seven Dwarfs (hardly a virgin after shacking up with seven horny little dudes in Jane Fonda tights).

We watched Father Knows Best, Leave It To Beaver and Donna Reed and began to shape and mold our future based on these "television families." Not only have these distortions been detrimental to Black women (we have been damaged the most because frankly, Black Americans watch more television) but they have been detrimental to all women who were led to believe that little girls grow up, learn to cook and sew, marry the boy next door, move into the house with the white picket fence, have a boy and a girl (in that order), become a housewife and mother and be happy for the rest of their lives.

We can criticize television, the system and anybody else but the truth of the matter is that in the midst of wanting their children to accept their poverty and tolerate their existence, a lot of Black parents neglected to help their children differentiate between what was possible and what was probable. Please don't misunderstand me. I'm not saying that living a comfortable, middle-class existence is beyond the grasp of many young black couples today. It most certainly isn't. But to believe that we—as a people—who were denied even the right to read and write for 100 years after we arrived here in America, who have been forced to live subhuman lives in a country our blood and sweat helped build, who have just begun to enter the mainstream of American life—could ever imitate the white man better than he imitates himself is ludicrous.

Black people have always been very, very good at imitating White folks. Starting in slavery when house niggers turned on field niggers, through reconstruction when "mulattoes" turned on darker-skinned Afro-Americans, to the twentieth-century where the bourgeoise have tried desperately to ignore the plight of the black poor.

But at some point, we have to stop the masquerade and take off the mask. At some point, we as Black women have to realize that if we want the "Father Knows Best" ideal of a man and husband and father for our children (where we greet him at the door at 5:00 in saran wrap), we're in trouble!

The reality of the situation is that what you see on television in White America and in books written by White men and women is not what the masses of Black Americans are going to get. What we have in reality is a nation of Black men—many of whom are reasonably intelligent, talented, mature and ambitious—but many of whom are the result of second or third generation angry black men and women riding a treadmill of undereducation, unemployment, crime, neglect, despair and all of the other evils born out of the burden of color.

Unfortunately, because of the severity and history of the race problem in America, many of these evils will not disappear when racial discrimination disappears (if ever). Unfortunately, there are many Americans—black and white—who believe that racism is so entwined into the fabric of American life that it will always be a part of our lives. While many of us (mostly diehard Christians) would like to believe that America will indeed "relieve" herself of the barnacles of racism, millions of other Americans disagree. They say that racism is here to stay, like foreign cars, fast food and AIDS.

Too many Black men and women have been too concerned with the race issue and have neglected the real problem—the death of the black family and how to get black men and black women together. The question is whether or not we should—based on the history of oppression and racism in this country—continue to walk in the shadows of the lie that we treat each other cruelly because America treats us cruelly. Can we continue to blame White America as we lie and cheat and beat each other out of our dignity, self-respect and stereos?

We must find the courage to see beyond what was and see the vision of what can be. We are third and fourth generation kings and queens. We are survivors. We survived African slavers, rat-infested ships, chains, beatings, rapes, murders, lynchings, burnings, the Klan and 39 presidents. I have no doubt we'll survive the crises of the eighties—hunger, unemployment and the never-ending search for love.

". . . more things belong in marriage than four bare legs in bed"

CHAPTER 4
_____

WHAT DO WOMEN WANT?

I don't know. If I could answer that, I'd be sipping Dom Perignone from 18K gold glasses and lighting the fireplace with one hundred dollar bills somewhere on the Ivory Coast.

What do I *think* most of us want? First and foremost, we want a man. Not just any man, mind you. Our man. The one that was promised us when we were little girls dreaming of ways to get out of the projects.

We want Mr. Right, Mr. Perfect and we want him to be Romeo, an Egyptian prince and a knight in shining armor. We want someone to love us and need us and protect us. What self-respecting woman doesn't want all of that rolled into one man and then more?

But what reasonably intelligent woman doesn't realize that men like that don't grow on trees (they certainly didn't grow on trees in my neighborhood) and in all likelihood, they don't exist except in our schoolgirl dreams.

In the real world, what we have are men who are reasonably attractive, reasonably intelligent, reasonably ambitious, reasonably romantic and thank God, reasonably sane. And because most women operate within these same "reasonable" limits, we should make perfect couples.

So why don't we? Probably because most women want quality and most men want quantity. Most women want the basics—health, wealth and happiness—preferably with the same person. We want a companion we can love, trust and respect (usually in that order). We want a man who brings more than a hard p-nis to a relationship (I warned you my language was frank). We want a man who is sensitive and warm and caring and understanding and supportive. We want someone who can feel love and sorrow and pity and is not ashamed to express it.

What else do we want? We want a satisfying job (if we have to work). We want to be a perfect size 8 and we want a good sex life (please GOD!). Yes, contrary to popular belief women like s-e-x. We like good s-e-x—not slam-bam-thank-you-mam s-e-x. We want someone who knows the difference between love and lust, making love and f--king. We want a man who understands that although some women enjoy being f--ked occasionally by someone they love, most of them prefer making love with someone they're f--king (We're all adults. Try to keep up please).

We want a love machine—not a sex machine. We want someone who cares if and when we "get ours" and when we don't. We want someone who doesn't make all of his decisions from his waist down and knows that if he shows just a little love and respect, he won't have to swindle us out of sex—it will be given freely.

We want a man who appreciates the strength, courage and tenacity of Black women and doesn't need a White woman to massage his ego and feed his insecurities. We want someone with at least a sprinkling of ambition, someone who doesn't worship material wealth but understands that money does have its place in a healthy, happy (and lasting) relationship. It's hard to be happy as a pig in sh-t when you're cold, hungry, homeless and in debt up to your navel.

We want a friend who appreciates our friendship and isn't driven to spending three or four nights a week with the boys to find someone who understands and appreciates him (so what am I . . . a paperweight?). We want a teacher, someone who is willing to teach us more about the things that bring us closer together—football, automobiles, changing a lightbulb. And we want someone who is equally as receptive to learning how to sew a button on his shirt, make a bed or cook a casserole.

We want someone who knows that "fetching and carrying" (i.e. the paper, the remote control, a glass of water) is a two-way street and women who work eight-hour days don't mind fetching and carrying if we know that someone will fetch and carry for us occasionally (who's counting?).

Frankly, we want someone who is tired of little boy games of pursue and conquer, one without a roving eye and one that doesn't feel that he needs a different woman every time he takes in a fresh supply of oxygen. We want a man who doesn't have to be taught that honesty is the best policy and that the best way to f--k up a decent relationship is to lie and f--k around.

We want a man who is not threatened by superficial things we might possess—a job, a car, a house—because he knows that all of us are a paycheck away from unemployment. We want a man who is secure enough to applaud our accomplishments and share our successes. We want a man with vision who not only encourages us to be the best but brings out the best in us because he knows that what's mine is his and vice versa and it can only get better.

What do women want? Simply to love and be loved by someone who wants to love and be loved.

What do women want? The same thing the Marines want . . . a few good men!

". . . women have to be and feel no more than what they are and no less than what they must be"

CHAPTER **5**

BUT WHAT DO WOMEN NEED?

The truth. Either you want us or you don't. Either you want to make it work or you don't. Either you're ready to settle down in a monogamous relationship or you're not.

What we don't need is a truckload of bullsh-t, particularly in the form of the big "L"—the almighty LIE—which is why I'm devoting an entire chapter to truth and honesty. These two words literally drop off the lips of women when they speak of priorities in a relationship. But they are the same two words that seem as foreign to men as taking the "pill" or changing sanitary napkins.

If you don't think that women put honesty right up there with love and sex and money, ask 100 women what has caused the most pain and grief in their relationships with the opposite sex. Nine out of ten will probably say dishonesty. For example, see if you're familiar with any of the ten more common lies either by association (or God forbid!) personal experience:

(1) "I'm not married" . . . although you see the imprint of a wedding band and guilt is dripping off his brow into his Courvosier.

(2) When asked "How did you get lipstick on your collar?", he replies "I don't remember. My secretary must have slipped and I caught her." . . . There are eight sets of lips on his shirt. Apparently the tramp needs brain surgery or a good chiropractor.

(3) "You know I love you, Baby!" . . . this may or may not be the truth depending on the time, the place and how hard he is. Have you noticed these six words are more frequently used while he's screwing you or after he's screwed up?

(4) "I don't know who she is!" . . . after he and some lady (I'm being kind) have danced the last nine dances and you've gotten wallpaper sores from standing in a corner fighting off creeps with b.o. at a party you didn't want to go to in the first place. He may not have known who she was when she came in but you can bet her fake Gucci bag, polyester pants and vinyl shoes that he'll know her name, number and favorite position before she leaves.

(5) "This has never happened to me before, Baby!" . . . after an unfortunate attempt to get it up. This has never happened to you before when? Yesterday? Last week? Since the sixth grade? What are you? The incredible hulk? Give me a break! We're both adults. You have a problem? Let's talk about it. It's not the end of the world unless you think with your p-nis and not your brain.

(6) "I'll call you tonight (or tomorrow)" . . . take your pick. This is a classic one. Sound familiar? These lines are usually spoken in passion or minutes after you've made out (more often than not at your home in your bed). Men

rarely say it when you leave them alone in their bed the morning-after. Something about being in their own domain that makes them feel they don't have to make any promises to anyone.

(7) "I stopped by a friend's house right after work and he didn't have a phone" . . . after getting off work at 5:00 and getting home at 2 a.m.. You have a friend that doesn't have a phone? What is he—the Neanderthal man? Everybody with lips has a phone! Try another one, please.

(8) "I'll be back in a few minutes. I'm going to get a pack of cigarettes." . . . Four hours later, he strolls in, empty-handed, smelling like a distillery and wonders why you're pissed.

(9) "I'll do it in a minute." . . . after you ask him to take out the garbage, pick up his stinky socks, hang up his shirt, take his plate off the table or wipe the toilet seat. (I gotta go now! Wipe the damn toilet seat!)

(10) This is my favorite. "She doesn't mean a damn thing to me! You're overreacting!" . . . after you've caught him having a drink in a bar with a half-naked girl 30 miles from home at 4:00 in the afternoon or God forbid, in your bed with a fully-naked girl when you decide to go home for lunch unexpectedly at noon.

The list goes on and on but soon they all begin to sound alike. The almighty lie! What can we do about it? Unfortunately, not much. The secret is to build a relationship with the kind of foundation that does not permit untruths to creep in and start chipping away at its strengths. Since most single women don't have those kinds of relationships (if we did, do you think we'd need this book?), perhaps we should start to look at the all-powerful lie somewhat differently.

First, if you are addicted to the truth (and a lot of women are), surely you know that telling the truth is still a novel experience for a lot of men. Habitual liars think that

15

(1) we believe everything they tell us and (2) they won't get caught. Based on these two assumptions, we can safely assume, therefore, that habitual liars suffer from an overdose of self-confidence. What's wrong with self-confidence? Nothing, if we use it to our advantage. If honesty is important to us, we should be as confident as he is that we won't be enslaved by liars or their lies.

If you've been deceived beyond a shadow of a doubt, confront him with it. If he denys it and you don't think you can ever forgive him, move on. It will take more courage to walk away than stay with him—not believing, not trusting, not loving. Believe me, the wound will heal, the pain will pass and you'll survive. And anyway, it's common knowledge that relationships don't work for people who don't want to work for them. So even if you believed he was "Mr. Right" momentarily, you're better off without him if you couldn't trust him!

". . . being male is a matter of birth. Being a man is a matter of choice."

CHAPTER 6

SOME THINGS MOTHER NEVER TOLD US

Most women in this country have been trained for dependency—not freedom. They have been taught that women should be helpless, hysterical creatures who need to be rescued from roaches, rats and flat tires. And although Black women have traditionally been the bread-winner and head-of-household, unfortunately some of us believe this garbage as well.

Somewhere we read that the logical progression in a woman's life is:

(1) Birth: A baby girl was a major disappointment to fathers in pre-historical days through the 19th century.

(2) School: To learn how to read recipes.

(3) Marriage: To make it legal and give him a steady dose of you-know-what.

(4) Motherhood: To prove his sperm are virile.

(5) Saint: When he starts screwing around.

(6) Martyr: When he dies and leaves no insurance.

(7) Death: The inevitable and usually a blessing after 50 years of numbers one through six.

Here are a few facts our mothers should have told us but didn't. It's not their fault for not telling us, however, because no one ever told them. Their mothers were too busy picking cotton, scrubbing Miss Ann's floors and breastfeeding Miss Sally's younguns.

(1) Stop playing the "I-don't-have-a-man-woe-is-me" blues. You do not have to feel illegitimate without a man. You are a child of God . . . a thinking, breathing child of God with your own soul and heart that beats independently of anyone else. Understandably, after years of misdirected energy and bizarre childish dreams, there is a conflict between wanting to be independent and wanting to depend on a man. But you cannot afford to allow the fear of being alone indefinitely retard your growth as a human being. Unfortunately some women have an unnatural fear that if we are alone, if we don't constantly have someone in our lives to reinforce our existence, we are nothing. This is by far the most ridiculous assumption I have ever heard.

Learning to love ourselves should be at the top of the list of our priorities. And when we learn that self-love is not conceit, that it is not a luxury, we will be one step closer to learning to love someone else. It's also easier to accept love (if it's good for you) or reject love (if it's not so good for you) if you feel good about yourself. And even more so if you're confident and secure with who you are. In short, if you feel bad about yourself, no man can make you feel good.

(2) Mother never told us that it's o.k. to enjoy s-e-x. Unfortunately, some women have not learned to separate love from sex. Love is spelled l-o-v-e and sex is spelled l-u-s-t. Many of us equate sex with love—intimacy and closeness. Most men see sex as sex. What most men won't (not don't) realize is that the best sex in the world is with someone you care about and someone who cares about you (hopefully they're the same person).

Unfortunately, most women are looking for love and romance and believe that sex is what you do to get love and romance. Some men, on the other hand, are looking for sex, and love and romance is what they must do to get sex. As you can see, therein lies one of the major problems facing single women today . . . a lack of communication.

How do we open up the lines of communication? First, we have to educate ourselves. We *must* develop a healthier attitude toward sex. Sex is easy to find (good sex is a little harder) but neither will do us any good if we have problems accepting our sexuality.

Many of us brought up in Christian environments (most Black women) find the search for companionship difficult for many reasons. Having people moving in and out of our lives at regular or irregular intervals can be very traumatic. Most of us have been taught that fornicating (polite language) is morally wrong and socially unacceptable. Thus having to fornicate with a new person every few months (sometimes every few weeks) insures us a seat in hell. But the idea of being alone starts to become even more appealing if fornication with a particular person time after time doesn't lead to a long-term relationship and commitment. We usually justify this infrequent but steady fornication by saying that "this time it's going to be real and may even lead to marriage" but soon wake up and realize that pipe dreams quickly come and go.

Many of us still look at sex as a gift that we give to men in exchange for services rendered . . . three-for-one drinks at

19

happy hour, a superficial conversation over dinner at a hole-in-a-wall or a phone call following the initial "act." Many of us still deny that we are also sexual beings, that many of us enjoy sex and that we would enjoy it even more if we had better sex.

And just as we take responsibility for what we eat for breakfast or wear to work everyday, we must learn to take responsibility for our sexual gratification. Taking responsibility can mean anything from taking the initiative when we see someone who turns us on and giving directions to the road leading to our gratification. Very seldom do men leave unsatisfied. Why should we?

(3) Mother (God bless her heart!) also forgot to tell us that sex without marriage does not cause insanity, sterility or pregnancy (at least not all of the time). Of course Mother couldn't have told us this. Many of us would have probably succumbed to our animal desires the first time a little boy rubbed our breasts, stuck his hands in our panties or demonstrated how dancing close made his third leg start to grow involuntarily. Many of us might have wound up with V.D. at fourteen, pregnant at fifteen and perhaps if we enjoyed it immensely, on the street at 16. So thank you Mother!

However, as we got older (18, 19 or 20) and we had no definite plans to go into a convent but were experiencing real physical needs, our mothers might have explained that perhaps (just perhaps) as growing girls, a little sex—now and then without benefit of marriage—just might be good for us. She might have told us that everytime you sleep with someone, you don't go shopping for a wedding ring the next morning. She might have mentioned that some people actually have sex to have pleasure and not babies (at least not all of the time).

Unfortunately, casual sex has such a bad reputation that when we meet someone halfway decent, we start tripping. "I want to 'do it' but if I 'do it' on the first date, he might think I'm easy. If I wait, he may not call again. But even if he calls again, how do I know he's not calling me because he really likes me or because he won't be satisfied until we 'do it'?" IT'S ENOUGH TO DRIVE YOU CRAZY!!!

The danger in this kind of "mind talk" is apparent. Why should you care more about the way he feels about you than the way you feel about yourself? The point is if you're attracted to him and he signs an affidavit that he doesn't have herpes or AIDS, why should you care what he thinks? You're single, he's single (I hope) and you don't live in a convent. Enjoy yourself. The point is to refuse to allow him to define you or become judge and jury for your actions. If you tried to read his mind or change your personality everytime a new person entered your life, you'd be schizophrenic and you wouldn't need a date . . . you'd need a caretaker!

I know that most of us like to feel that there is at least the potential of a relationship before we sleep with someone but, alas, life has no guarantees. If he never calls again, forget him. As soon as you can accept the fact that he was not **your** PRINCE Charming (if he were, he'd still be there), the sooner you can get on with your life and rid yourself of the anxieties, fears and insecurities that threaten our growth. It should also occur to you that if he never calls again, it might be a blessing in disguise. You should thank the Lord for sparing you four or five months of agony over someone who never had any intention of fulfilling your wildest dreams.

Unfortunately, there is no foolproof way to weed out the men who only want a one-night stand from the ones who are looking for an honest relationship. Many of them are so protective of their emotions, so careful not to reveal who they really are, that what they say and what they do may be in direct conflict. He may whisper sweet nothings in your ear for two weeks straight and then never call again. He may send you cards and flowers everyday at the office for a week, sleep with you on Friday night and disappear. Again, there are no guarantees.

So unless you're extremely careful and get to know yourself first, and most importantly, determine what you want out of the encounter and how much you're willing to give and take, you may wind up in a series of unfulfilled affairs that leave you emotionally chained to feelings of confusion, guilt and hopelessness.

But I wouldn't knock a little confusion, guilt and hopelessness. All three have helped us find out—the hard way—that love and sex are two different words. Believe me, it hasn't been easy and it hasn't been fun. After our share of sexual derelicts and other forgettables, many of us wanted to give up. We found out that there are people you should follow anywhere but to the bedroom. We also found out that even those you followed to the bedroom, you shouldn't always sleep with.

As we pursued our pursuer, he was usually in pursuit of pure and simple pleasure, without a second thought to our emotional well-being. So those of us who had broken sexual revolution barriers and made a conscious decision to at least "experiment" with sex without becoming too promiscuous (is that possible?), soon began to have doubts about sex for sex's sake (is that a song?).

Granted, our mothers didn't teach us everything we ever wanted to know about sex but they taught most of us an equally important lesson . . . IT'S OUR THANG! and we can do what we want to do with it! And with that bit of knowledge tucked away in our conscience, we began to realize that sex for sex's sake was o.k. if you know what you're doing (how many of us really do?). Sex for sex's sake was o.k. if you didn't write little fairy tales with happy endings for men who were not only unable to commit but unwilling.

22

Sex for sex's sake was o.k. if you weren't allowing yourself to become a victim of some of the astringent a--holes who suffer emotional paralysis everytime they find themselves becoming more than just a little attached to a woman. Sex for sex's sake was o.k. if you realized that oftentimes women are underdogs in such encounters but it's o.k. to be the underdog if you're a smart underdog. If he insists on giving you crumbs, take them if you want them and get the hell out! But don't allow him to give you crumbs if you really want a whole slice of bread. Tell him "thank you but no thank you" and get the hell out!

Your decision to experience sex without love is just that—your decision. Some of us can do it, some of us can't. Regardless of how you use sex or let sex use you, your ultimate goal should be to find the situation that makes you feel comfortable. And to do that, you have to know who you are, what you want and what you're willing to do to get it (I plan to say this at least ten more times).

". . . life is what passes you by while you're making other plans"

CHAPTER 7
_____

A THEORY

I wrote this book for two very selfish reasons:
(1) I'm concerned about my future and my continued personal growth if I remain unmarried and

(2) I'd like to make a million dollars and move to the Virgin Islands. (Honesty is the best policy, isn't it?)

Beyond those two reasons, I wrote the book to share with whoever reads it what I believe is the solution to some of the problems that haunt all single women in their relationships with the opposite sex.

If you read the first few chapters (some people skip to the juicy part), you probably have already noticed that I talk a lot about sex. I'm not preoccupied with sex but I believe that most of the problems we face as women in relationships stem from the manner we have been taught to deal with sex. Traditionally, most women have viewed sex as something sacred, to be brought out, dressed up and given away at Christmas, Valentine's Day and let's not forget those Sunday afternoon surprises for men who just by their presence in our lives have "earned it" and therefore "deserve it".

If you don't already know by now that *nobody* deserves it unless *you* want to *give* it to them, then I'm really glad you bought this book!

It's your body, dammit! It belongs to you and no one else. Nobody else has the right to abuse it or misuse it. When you allow other people to come into your life and "take charge" of your body, including your emotions, for even a short period of time, you have given up the most important God-given right you possess—your right to choose. Your right to choose what's good or bad for you and what's in your best interest.

It's unfortunate that many women find it difficult—for whatever reasons—to take charge of their lives. Some of us are still afraid to let our voices be heard—particularly on issues that only we should be addressing, like our sexuality. At thirty or forty or even fifty years of age, some of us are still afraid to openly express our sexuality for fear that someone might conclude that most of us enjoy sex. The truth is that we do enjoy it and we would enjoy it even more if men would become more skillful lovers and take the time to satisfy our needs (but that's another book!)

We are ashamed of our bodies if we have a few extra pounds here and there, particularly if we are well-endowed in the hip and thigh areas. Women of color are very shapely, sensuous women but many of us are so obsessed with the European standard of beauty (five foot six, dress size six, shoe size six, six inch waist, six inch breasts, etc. etc. etc.) that we have forgotten the unique beauty of the African woman. Why then are we constantly trying to force our size ten or twelve frames into size six designer jeans that are obviously not sewn for us? Have we forgotten that our near-perfect breasts and bountiful hips are envied all around the world? If our men refuse to accept us and our bodies as second generation African women, then they deny their own heritage—their own thick noses, full lips, ashy skin, razor bumps, thin unshapely but strong legs and, I might add, their tight, curved little asses.

Apparently many of us haven't learned to appreciate these physical differences and therefore haven't learned to express our sexuality fully. Not that we should ever go completely into left field and lose all sense of morality like some other people we know (wife swapping, group sex, mating with monkeys, etc.) but at least we ought to feel less inhibited and more comfortable about "the act" in the privacy of our own (or someone else's) bedroom.

The question of our sexuality, however, often leads us back to our own men. Because the good girl-bad girl syndrome is so vague and confusing, we don't completely trust our men with our emotions (forget our bodies). So if we think about "getting down" whenever the mood strikes us, we still seek their approval more often than we explore our own feelings and act accordingly. It's the eighties, you're in charge and the sky's the limit. Go for it!

* * * *

The other major obstacle in our pursuit of happiness with a man is the fact that most of us are not looking for *just* a relationship. We want a *real* relationship. We want an exclusive relationship. We want to date only the "marriageables" just in case we decide to marry him. Unfortunately, with the shortage of "acceptable" men (more about them later), this may not always be possible. In fact, it may be downright impossible.

The only statistic that has changed drastically in the last ten years in male-female relationships has been the increase in divorce and the decrease in marriages and babies. If fewer people are getting married and even fewer are involved in exclusive relationships, where does the single woman who wants to get married fit in? What does she have to look forward to? What the hell is the problem?

The answers to those questions are simple. She fits in where she wants to fit in, she has a helluva lot to look forward to and the problem, in a nutshell, is her. Why? Because some of us refuse to take responsibility for our own happiness. Because far too many of us still have stars in our eyes from too many Harlequin romances and Rock Hudson movies (did I say that?). Too many of us see what we want to see and nothing else. What are we *really* missing if we're not involved, if we're going through life solo at the moment?

Let's examine the basic male-female relationship:

STAGE 1:   The initial stage is primal sex . . . f---ing . . . whatever you feel comfortable calling it. It is still sex for sex's sake. Men have been doing it for centuries (women have too but usually got paid for it). Many of us brought up in the church or with low sex drives frown on f---ing for f---ing sake. We think it's cheap, degrading and if you have any morals, you aren't supposed to enjoy it and you have to feel guilty the morning after.

Thousands of women have made the adjustment to the male shortage by making a conscious decision not to do without sex although they may have to do without a steady boyfriend.

They f--k on a regular basis, oftentimes with people they like but are not in a "relationship" with and sometimes with people they don't particularly dislike but are satisfied with their skill in bed. Some of these same women make out with strangers on a regular basis. I personally don't think it's safe but these women have made their choice—they know what they want and how to get it. Nevertheless, I think it's safe to say that a great majority of women still have problems with sex for sex's sake. So the password in Stage 1 is *sex*.

STAGE 2: The next stage is limited dating. In this stage, you occasionally go to a movie, maybe even go to dinner or drinks (but never in a club where he takes the risk of running into some of his friends who might assume he has a "regular.") The foundation of this relationship is usually based on sex but the fringe benefits—dinner, movies, booze—are pleasant frills so "good" girls don't feel as guilty the morning-after. Either of you may be seeing someone else but the topic is never brought up. You know you aren't the only one in his life but you can live without the gory details.

You simply let it flow. Sex is good, you enjoy each other and your self-esteem is left intact. Limited dating includes—but is not limited to—newly acquired male friends, ex-boyfriends, ex-husbands (if you can stand them), married men (more about them later), long distance romances, etc. The password in Stage 2 is *availability*.

STAGE 3, simply stated, is "a relationship." A combination of more frequent contact, more intimate and in-depth conversations, steady dates, improved sex and of course, more disagreements (everyone knows that the more you see of one another, the more you can be your "other" self). Some women refer to this stage as a "real" relationship but whatever you choose to call it, in this stage you get more of everything because both of you are not afraid to give more. The password, therefore, is *more*.

STAGE 4: The next stage is the ultimate—the cream of the crop—the exclusive relationship. Me for you and you for me. If I get herpes, I know you must have given it back to me and I must have gotten it from a toilet seat since neither of us is sleeping with anyone else. Right? In this stage, there is less "dating" (getting dressed and going out) but more time together and more sharing of one's space, of one's dreams and goals, more vacations together and long-range plans (anything beyond the weekend is long-range plans for some men). The key word in an exclusive relationship is *trust*.

STAGE 5:   The final stage in the male-female relationship (this side of divorce) is of course marriage, the ultimate commitment. (Living together doesn't count.) Your wildest dreams come true. He is not only available but accessible. Marriage—the ultimate in love, sex, bad breath and ring around the collar. What more could you ask for? The password here is *luck* although *love* is the real key.

"... you can give without loving but you cannot love without giving"

CHAPTER **8**

BUT WHAT IS LOVE?

Hell if I know!

". . . love is love's reward"

CHAPTER **9**

WHAT I THINK LOVE IS

There are many different kinds of love but since you obviously didn't spend $7.95 to find out how to fall in love with your microwave, let's talk about the love between a man and a woman—romantic love, intimate love, love love!

Love, simply stated, is something you *do*—not something you *say!* Love is one of life's strongest emotions, right up there with fear and hate. Love is elusive to those who do not understand that it can't be bought or sold. You can't grow it in a pot or borrow it from a friend. Cupid prowls around the street day and night looking for potential lovers but he doesn't always do a very good job of screening them (sorry Cupid, the truth hurts!) Cupid makes a lot of boo-boos but he'll probably only take credit for creating opportunities for people to *meet* and *fall* in love—not *stay* in love.

Cupid says love is blind. I say it shouldn't be. We are so afraid of that great void in our lives that we mistake a few laughs, a good screw and two phone calls in the same day as love. And too many of us have love addictions—in and out of affairs, looking for love in all of the wrong places to satisfy our addiction. We don't want to be alone so it doesn't matter that we're not traveling the same path as he or that he's shallow, preoccupied with self and too obsessed with his own frail ego to return that love. It doesn't matter that we were ten times happier alone than we are "in love" or that the only thing you really have in common is that you both desire to make *him* happy!

I thought I was in love only once in my life. Surprisingly, it was not until after we went our separate ways that I began to imagine that I loved him. But I've never thought of love as a solo act and his self-esteem was so low and he was still so bitter about his divorce that even two years later, he had not fully recovered. Eventually whatever I felt for him took a back seat to my love for myself because I knew that God did not intend for me to mourn the loss of our relationship forever as He had not intended for my friend to mourn the loss of his marriage indefinitely. So after deep soul searching, I voluntarily said goodbye.

How many of us are haunted by the memories of bad or unproductive relationships? How many of us have not allowed those memories to fade into oblivion and be happy that we were brave and strong enough to move on? Your mistakes will only haunt you if you allow them to do so. Most of us give a bad relationship the power to hurt us again and again, to sap our energy and cloud our vision. Why is it so difficult to remember that it's our life, that we have a right to let things in when they make us happy and get rid of those things and people that make us unhappy?

We have to learn to let go and remember that a man is an option—like a sunroof or power windows on a new car. Even without the luxuries, you still have the key, your engine will still turn over and all you have to do is put it in drive and get on with your life.

Sometimes people say that you never recover from your first love. In a way, that may be true. But if you understand that a healthy relationship demands growth and change, you will not allow ghosts of past relationships to interfere with the birth of a new relationship. If you don't understand this simple fact and refuse to allow a previous relationship to die a natural death (and be buried), then you're always going to be in the "limited dating" stage. If that's where you want to be, fine. But if you want more (and most of us do), move on.

What is love?

I would not be so egotistical as to define it for you but to me. . . .

Love is romance and passion, loyalty and trust, patience and tolerance.

Love is a chance at the happiness some of us won't take time to find within ourselves.

Love is two grown people acting like they can't do without each other until they find someone else.

Love, my friend, is truly a trip!

. . . but long live love!

". . . if the cake is bad, what good is the frosting?"

CHAPTER **10**

UNDESIRABLES
(AUTOMATIC ELIMINATIONS)

Although we hate to admit it (until after we've been dumped on), love is more than just an emotion. Unfortunately, the heart frequently speaks louder than logic or common sense. We meet someone, he turns us on. The heart beats overtime and the brain takes a coffee break. It doesn't matter if you have absolutely nothing in common with each other, that he picks his nose in public or that he hasn't had a steady job since he was 16. You like him, he likes you and that's all that matters. BULL!

Even if you hate putting labels on people, there are some men that single women should avoid like the plague (or AIDS). Men who may be available but are simply "undesirable" and should be "automatically eliminated" from your "acceptable" list.

37

For example, if looking in the mirror the morning-after is a traumatic experience, you've probably spent the night with an undesirable. Sharing your bed, your heart and the most intimate secrets of your body and soul with an undesirable who still looks like an undesirable in the morning (bad breath and all) is masochistic. Even if you love yourself, feelings of self-contempt and self-hatred can creep up, whisper in your ear and get you down.

The secret is to provide enough love and warmth and kindness and understanding and positive reinforcement to *yourself* that even when huge black clouds follow you around for days or even weeks after an encounter with an undesirable (whether it's a mental or physical encounter), you will be confident the clouds will pass, the sun will shine and your life will go on.

The secret is to remember that you are the producer, director and star of your own life. It is your drama (or comedy) and your ultimate goal should be to survive (and thrive) with or without a man. When you learn to be a powerbroker in your own life, you learn to make your own decisions. And when you learn to make your own decisions, you decide who you are, what you want and what you accept or reject in your life.

And speaking of rejection, since a lot of women are practicing masochists (don't look surprised!), this take-charge-of-my-life attitude may be difficult to adjust to in the beginning. First, you've got to answer some very important questions.

(1) What do I really want?

(2) What don't I want?

(3) Where can I compromise?

Curiously enough, most of us can't fully define or describe what we want but we'll tell you in a New York minute what we don't want. Most of us know, for example, that just because a man is "available" doesn't mean he's "acceptable" as a potential companion or mate. To help those of you who don't know the difference between *available* and *acceptable*, I've compiled a list of men who I believe should be automatically eliminated from your list of prospects if you are seriously interested in beginning and/or maintaining a healthy, meaningful, long or short-term relationship. It's purely subjective (but so is this book) so if you have been certified as a masochist and have no desire to change, you may skip this chapter:

(1) Known homosexuals: Although these dainty darlings imitate us better than we do ourselves and make very good dancers, artists and friends, trying to initiate or maintain anything other than a platonic relationship with one of them is like trying to get the Pope to admit that as a child, he lusted for someone of the opposite sex. The exception is, of course, not knowing that your very sensitive, very clean-cut, earring-wearing sweetie is a homosexual going through an identity crisis and trying to pass as a heterosexual.

If you are one of the unfortunate ones and find out after you've gone out a few times and maybe even "made out," the first thing you don't do is blame yourself. It is not a question of your sexuality but a statement of his struggle. Reflect on a few positive moments in your short-term relationship (you may have to look under a rock) and move on. A person who loves herself does not blame herself for someone else's decision not to have the very best—her.

Footnote: Aren't you tired of well-meaning friends spotting a hunk who is obviously gay and saying something self-defeating like "what a waste?" I suggest that if this brother had homosexual tendencies and you found out six months after your relationship started, it would be more of a waste. Don't always think the grass is greener (or even straighter) on the other side. And if that's not enough to set her straight, remind her that if he is that much of a hunk, if he were straight, he probably wouldn't talk to *her* anyway! (This is war, go for the juggler vein and help save her self-esteem.)

(2)   Closet Homosexuals: Avoid these guys for basically the same reasons mentioned in number one except you have to be very alert to recognize some of them. Many of them lift weights, play football and make babies.

(3)   Bisexuals: These are greedy S.O.B.s. They want to straddle the fence . . . and you . . . and the quarterback . . . and your ex-boy friend . . . etc. But once again, they are very hard to recognize sometimes. Keep your eyes and instincts open, particularly since AIDS follows him around like a shadow.

(4)   Asexuals: Unless you don't give a damn about sex in a male-female relationship (or plan to enter a convent later in life), stay clear of these guys. They are usually very sweet but if you're horny, all they can do is suggest a cold shower.

(5)   Drug Addicts and Pushers: These sh-theads are so obviously a waste of time, they don't deserve a whole paragraph. Anyone who doesn't give a damn about himself or the kids he sells drugs to, doesn't deserve me. It's just that simple. In fact, you could use some of the energy you spend worrying about being single to help get some of these dopes off the streets! (You've got to be a dope to put a stinking needle in your vein or pay $300 for a bag of sh-t that you snort like a pig!)

All of the rhetoric in the world could not possibly convince me that a drug addict loved me. How could he possibly love me when he unmistakably does not love himself? And if that's not bad enough, he'd probably trade you for a joint or a kilo anyday.

In short, drug addicts and pushers are too selfish and have too little regard for human life. And if that's not enough, all of them are usually impotent on or off drugs.

(6)   Alcoholics: These guys are another no-no. I know that alcoholism is a disease and I sympathize with anyone who has a disease. But I also know that a lot of women enjoy impersonating Florence Nightingale when we meet an alcoholic. We quickly forget that there is little we can do for him if he won't help himself. We inevitably believe that we can get to the root of the problem, drive him to AA meetings three times a week and live happily (and soberly) ever after.

The truth is (1) very few of us are trained to counsel real alcoholics (2) nine times out of ten you will probably suffer more than he does during his binges and (3) unless he wants to stop drinking, he never will. This is not to say that you should completely write off this hope chest of "available" men. Just proceed with caution. If you fall in love with an alcoholic, don't stop loving yourself. If he doesn't reform, at least you still have a lover around—yourself. An additional note: If you fall in love with an alcoholic, get ready for expensive liquor bills, some violence, wet toilet seats and impotence (even when they're sober).

(7)   All-around Bastards: In one sentence, leave these crazy bimbos alone! Occasionally, some of us unwittingly get involved with men who must show their superiority by kicking a--, preferably ours. Just for the record, this is totally unacceptable for women who love themselves. If you allow this madman to take out his fears and insecurities on you, you are giving him "the power" that is rightfully yours to determine who is in control of your life and who determines what's good and what's not-so-good for you.

We simply can't spend a lifetime playing nurse to these insecurities, patching ourselves back up and making excuses for his failure to grow up. A good relationship depends on the mature and emotional well-being of each of you. If he is unable (or unwilling) to meet the challenges of being a "grownup" and insists on nurturing his destructive behavior and reverting to typical adolescent scenes like having fits and kicking your a-- to "feel better" about himself, your decision to leave him should be a relatively easy one. Just get rid of the crazy SOB! It's him or you! It's as simple as that.

How can anyone who professes to love me give me black eyes, break my arms and pour hot grease down my pantyhose? Apparently, we speak a different language and one of us doesn't know what "love" means (and it ain't me!). Besides, hospital and cosmetic bills can be astronomical and unless you're kinky, love is not a violent act. Footnote: "If a dog bites you, it's his fault. If he bites you again, it's your fault." Anyway, everyone knows that men who beat women are wimps and usually have small penises.

(8)   Certified Mentally Unbalanced Men (CMUM): A lot of CMUM (pronounced cum) haven't been certified but little doubt remains after you spend a few minutes with them. You can be sympathetic and caring but get deeply emotionally involved at your own risk. Without constant medical attention and treatment, many of them may eventually fall off the deep end, wind up in a strait jacket, kill themselves or you.

How do you recognize CMUM? If he frequently stares into space, loses his concentration most of the time, disappears for days, can't explain his absences and always looks as though he were ready to slice your throat, you probably have a CMUM on your hands. If you're already attached to him but still have doubts about his sanity, give him a Valium and have some tissue samples taken from his brain. If the results come back stamped "MADE BY MATTEL FOR CHILDREN UNDER THREE," run— not walk—to the nearest airport or train station and ask for a one-way ticket.

(9)   The Walking Wounded: These are men who have been divorced for less than two years, particularly those who didn't have a choice in the matter (they were filed on) or whose wives played around on them (they'll never admit it). The walking wounded are usually very bitter and it's very difficult to find out why at the beginning. Sometimes it's because they wanted the marriage to work. Sometimes it's because they didn't file first (juvenile isn't it?) Sometimes it's because his ego can never forgive his ex-wife's indiscretion (affair) so the rest of us have to pay for it in installments for the remainder of our natural lives.

If you choose to date one of the walking wounded, wear heavy armor to protect yourself, particularly around your heart. Women usually find it relatively easy to love the walking wounded because they are vulnerable, lonely, despondent and reach out to anyone who is reasonably nice and will listen to them refer to their ex-wife as "my wife" ten or twelve times during the course of your first, second and even third date. After awhile—no matter how much you care about this man—when he starts talking about his ex-wife, you want to tell him to "SHUT THE F--K UP!" particularly if you're in the middle of a lovemaking session.

Although the walking wounded have a desperate need for companionship, they are usually unprepared for the big C—commitment (some of them can't even say the word). Many are still in shock, angry and weave in and out of moodiness through an invisible revolving door. In short, the first woman in a walking wounded's life has a thankless job—a modern-day Florence Nightingale who wears his pain and grief as your uniform until he recovers . . . if he ever does.

If you recognize the symptoms going into a relationship with the walking wounded and can hang in, you've made yourself a wonderful friend. They will always be eternally grateful for your patience and you probably have a friend for life. However, once they recover, they start the search for "Miss Right" and you may have lost a lover and a friend. Footnote: Be careful not to fall in love with too many of the walking wounded in your lifetime. Although a few of them are a little "crazy" (confused may be a better word), some of them may be "catching" and you'll never get them out of your system. In short, they may be hazardous to your continued mental and emotional well-being. You simply can't afford to be in love with someone who doesn't love you. Case closed.

(10) The Chronically Unemployed: Because of the economic recession and the current administration's inability or desire to address the problem of massive unemployment, automatically eliminating the chronically unemployed from our list of desirables may piss off a lot of people reading this book. So how do you tell the difference between a brother who's worked for 15 years for an oil tool company and was laid off in the crunch from a brother who hasn't had a job in 15 years and doesn't give a sh-t about gainful employment?

Easy. Impersonate Sherlock Holmes. Ask questions. Give him a lie detector test if necessary. Listen to his rap. See where his head is. Open your eyes. It shouldn't be difficult to identify Mr. Do Nothing, Be Nothing and Have Nothing. He'll be doing nothing, being nothing and having nothing.

If you can accept his lack of ambition or drive or whatever you want to call it, then so be it. If it doesn't bother you that your man doesn't get up and get dressed and go to work every morning and bring home some of the bacon at least some of the time, more power to you. But if it never crosses your mind, I'd do a little self-examination. Why isn't his self-worth important to you? Some studies indicate that a man's self-esteem and self-worth—for better or worse—are unmistakably tied to his employment. If the studies are accurate, it must be very difficult for a man who is chronically unemployed *by choice* to have good self-esteem.

The question then becomes why are you turned on to this spineless, gutless do nothing? *You* may have a problem. His choice not to work and your being able to accept it makes a statement about him and you (but again, who am I to question it?)

(11) Criminals (both active and inactive): First, if they're really active, pray that the cops will arrest them before you become too involved with them. We all know that a disproportionate number of Black men are in prisons and that many of them are there because of a history of racism and prejudice in our judicial system. But lest we forget and think that all of the brothers in prison are innocent, let's remember what comedian Richard Pryor said after visiting one of our state institutions . . . "THANK GOD WE GOT PRISONS!"

When you become lonely and desperate and think of penpaling with an inmate, try to remember these three facts:

(1) Long distance love is usually *no* love at all, (particularly when he's up for life)

(2) If he's *not* on death row or up the river for life, Mr. Bic will get out one day and

(3) *When* he gets out, you'd better pray he was one of the *innocent* ones!

This, of course, does not mean deserting solid lovers who are arrested in the midst of a good relationship (a good relationship with a man who steals televisions from little old ladies?) In those instances, you have to examine your needs to determine if you are willing to make the sacrifices necessary to be his "moll" after he gets out (24-hour stakeouts, bars on the living room window, etc.)

As far as ex-convicts (ex-inmates) are concerned, if you follow your instinct it shouldn't be difficult to decide if your friend plans to walk a straight line after he gets out of prison. If he does, he may be a perfect mate for you. He'll appreciate his freedom and probably do anything to protect it. On the other hand, if he gives you subtle hints that he doesn't plan to mend his ways (dancing with a sawed-off shotgun, wearing a mask to work or sleepwalking in banks at 3 AM in the morning) you might want to reconsider your decision to give him another chance. By the way, don't be ashamed to say you've changed your mind. Better late than never because if he appears to be too hot to handle, he probably is. Drop him!

(12)   Emotional Cripples: Years of dependency on other people (usually their sadistic mothers or other women who feed off their illness) have made these men undesirables. Again, heartfelt sympathy and concern are in order but long-term relationships with these men should be avoided at all costs.

(13)   Black men with the pink lady complex: These are men who are preoccupied with white women . . . the "forbidden fruit freaks" . . . who are looking for their stolen identity in the white man's bed. . . who need a constant reminder of the black sexuality myth (I refuse to support or deny this rumor!).

For years, sisters have tolerated or tried to ignore these men (actually they only represent 1% of the Black men in this country). It's been a very difficult pill to swallow particularly since the man shortage has become more apparent since the Vietnam War. Thousands of decent Black men were killed during that senseless slaughter and many who returned are still suffering from the trauma.

Even today, many of us—particularly if we're single—still stare at interracial couples. We still get angry if he's good-looking and she's a dog (nine times out of ten). And unfortunately, many of us begin to question our own femininity and believe the "black-women-castrate-their-men" myth.

In one word . . . don't! Don't stare! Don't question! And for God's sake . . . don't get angry! His decision to sleep with (or date or marry or whatever) white women has absolutely nothing to do with you personally. Don't nurse your hatred or resentment of the black/white thing. This racist attitude can be a handicap in your attempt to find personal satisfaction and happiness in your own life. If the black male/white female union is your demon, tell him to get lost. A negative attitude about something over which you have no control is too destructive. Anyway, Black men who exclusively date and marry White women are usually gay, impotent or have small penises (sometimes all three).

There are many other undesirables (nerds, turds, geeks, freaks, etc.), far too numerous to mention here but I think you catch my drift.

". . . you meet a lot of guys but very few men"

CHAPTER **11**

REAL MEN

How can you tell the difference between an undesirable and a "real man"? I thought you'd never ask!

A real man is sensitive, caring, gentle, thoughtful and respectful (not necessarily in that order and not all of the time but at least he tries).

A real man remembers birthdays, anniversaries and holidays. He's heard of a telephone when he's an hour late for dinner. He helps his woman do *their* housework (he has nothing to prove so he doesn't care if his buddies see him cooking or doing laundry).

A real man who knows nothing about repairing the toaster, the lawnmower and the car doesn't think twice about calling an electrician, a gardner or a mechanic.

A real man is secure enough to understand that a plane needs co-pilots. He not only admires you for making decisions in your partnership but respects your right to do so.

A real man doesn't leave dirty socks and stiff shorts all over the restroom because his "fairy godmother" will levitate by and pick them up.

A real man knows that men and women sometimes have to use the same toilet and if women (and men occasionally) hadn't needed the toilet seat, God wouldn't have put it on top of the toilet!

Real men still open and close doors to cars, not because they have to but because they want to. They don't believe all of that crap about women not wanting them to open doors, light cigarettes and send flowers (undesirables probably started those ridiculous rumors).

Real men seldom lie but even when they do, people they love usually don't get hurt.

A real man is not afraid to say "no" or hear "no." He's not afraid to apologize or say "I'm sorry" because he knows that admitting a mistake makes him an even bigger man.

A real man is never an atheist. He believes in God because he is not foolish enough to believe that "the world appeared by itself" or that he had anything to do with it.

A real man does not forsake his woman for his male friends or hide his woman from his female friends. If he goes out with the boys, he doesn't have to rap to the girls to prove anything to the boys.

A real man does not get physical except in the gym or on the basketball court. He believes that only raccoons should have black eyes and only trees should have broken limbs.

A real man has a dream. He is ambitious and appreciates a good job, a nice car and a beautiful home but understands that all of these material things cannot replace a good woman, a good lover, a good friend. He gives abundantly because he knows he will receive abundantly.

When a real man loves a woman, he cares if she gets hers before he gets his. He knows that sex without love is so-so but that sex with love is the ultimate. A real man knows that sex without love gets old so he takes the time to find out what satisfies his woman. He also knows in most instances—including sex—haste makes waste. (Think about it!)

Real men know that romance is the bread of life and even if they are not romantic by nature, they know that an unexpected kiss or hug (without pawing) is always appreciated and usually well-rewarded (in more ways than one).

A real man needs space and gives space to people he cares about or loves. He is not afraid to say "I love you" or "I need you" to someone he loves and needs.

A real man has a conscience and knows the pain of a lie and the power of the truth.

A real man is a friend and lover to his friend and lover.

A real man, in a nutshell, is not afraid of a real woman.

". . . greener pastures often have higher fences around them"

CHAPTER **12**

WHERE TO MEET REAL MEN

ANYWHERE YOU CAN!

". . . there is no shame in not knowing, only in refusing to learn"

CHAPTER **13**

WHAT MEN MUST LEARN

Our men must learn that they are human, that we all have frailties and we all make mistakes. Unfortunately, most men belong to a secret society and have been taught from birth to be macho, not to show their feelings and for God's sake, don't cry!

Today women bear the burden of this stone-age mentality. We have to feed fiberglass egos, so fragile that they shatter if we get them to admit that they care about us even a little bit. Nine times out of ten we have to decipher what they really mean when they don't say what they wish they could??? (you figure that one out. Confusing isn't it?)

I want to believe that our men want to be touched and held and kissed without making love *all* of the time but are oftentimes afraid to express it. Society says that if you touch and hug and kiss, a woman might confuse you with a human being and even assume that you want to enjoy her company as well as her body.

So what do you do? You touch, you hug, you kiss and then you *always* (let me repeat) *always* make out even if all you wanted was a simple kiss. Their confusion becomes your confusion. Their conflict, your conflict. The question then becomes "Since what society says is more important to you than what you or I want or feel, why not make out with society instead of me?"

Our men must learn to be honest with themselves and with us. Either you want me or you don't. Black men have been exploited but so have Black women. The truth is that Black women are still at the bottom of the socio-economic ladder in America and more often than not, non-voting members of the black male-black female relationship as well.

Our men must learn to flush that European macho bullsh-t down the toilet before they come to us with their arms open, looking for love and tenderness. They must learn that they can't have everything (who can?) and that only God has the right to play with other people's lives.

We have learned—through years of practice—to tolerate inconsiderate, infantile behavior in relationships. Rather than cancel a date or end a relationship like a real man, many of them disappear after one date and fade into the woodwork. They make vacant promises and empty, unfilled vows to be faithful and rather than face the "singles plague," we love-starved little kittens continue to allow this anti-social behavior of lies covering up lies to carve our hearts into tiny little pieces to be chewed up and spit out again and again.

Frankly, I think one of our problems is that we make rational demands on irrational human beings. We talk to our men as if we actually know what makes them tick. We don't. We try hard and we think we do but we don't (and probably never will).

Most of them—like us—are wearing masks to hide the anger, the hurt, the disappointment, the disillusionment with ourselves, with each other and with life. We can blame everything from misplaced values to racism but frankly, the solution to our problems lies a lot closer to home—within ourselves.

We can criticize the system but it is we who—time after time—in search of the perfect mate, attach ourselves to undesirables, to men of little substance, to superficial sambos, to men with self-destructive impulses who carry us along with them to the brink of pain and disaster.

Some of us are so obsessed with marriage, so pre-occupied with a "relationship," that we neglect to be content with what we already have. We forget that it's o.k. to be single. (I didn't say it was good or bad but simply o.k.) Some of my most creative and most productive moments occur when I am alone, marching to a different drummer or mapping out my life. And anyway, haven't you heard? The grass is not always greener on the other side (ask some of your married friends . . . a few might tell you the truth).

(3) And finally our men must learn that there are no more "mammies" (although very few of us would have survived without strong black women in our history). Our men must learn that although racial equality is and has been a top priority for all of Black America, sexual parity cannot be ignored.

Why? Because Black women are also beaten and raped and victimized. Because Black women have always had to play mommy and daddy. Because Black women are still being blamed for the scarcity of jobs in the Black community. Isn't it sad that some of our men get angry at us because we have been able to get and keep jobs (screw the reasons) to support *their* children and *them* if necessary? To say that Black women are liberated and shouldn't be concerned about women's rights is downright ridiculous!

Our men must learn that a male-dominated world will soon be obsolete. Too many women have had to work too long and too hard for what little happiness and success we enjoy. We have come to a point in our lives that we should refuse to allow anyone—male or female, black or white—to set up a detour or build a brick wall to stop us from achieving even more. We love our men (I know I do) and we'd like to share our successes with them. But if they won't allow us to, we'll go it alone!

". . . it's better to build children than repair men"

CHAPTER **14**

ENEMY #1

Women have been taking risks for years. The risk of loving without being loved, the risk of rejection and certainly the risk of becoming pregnant. Men, on the other hand, have historically been on top (literally). They make the decisions, they make the choices, they call the shots. So why are they so afraid? What are they afraid of?

Besides herpes, a small penis and temporary impotence, I personally believe that a lot of men are simply afraid of being afraid. They're afraid of fear. Fear has become their number one enemy. They're afraid of loving . . . afraid of not being loved . . . afraid of closeness . . . afraid of too much space. Afraid of sex without love and love without sex.

"WAIT!" you say. "That last statement can't be true!" "Did you say that men are afraid of love without sex and sex without love?" I most certainly did. Most women would probably agree that a lot of men ultimately just want to "get off" but along the way, those same men want their egos inflated as well. They want you to care enough about them to make the "ultimate sacrifice" (next to having their baby) and that's dropping your drawers. They want to feel that you don't "do it" with everybody and anybody. They want to feel special (who doesn't?). And since we're on the subject, whether or not you're satisfied physically has nothing to do with (1) his satisfaction (2) his ego or (3) his need to be important to you. That's a separate issue entirely and one we will discuss later in this book.

Although very few men will admit it for fear of sounding human, men *want* and *need* more than just sex. Let me explain that even further. A real man (you read about him earlier), one with a working conscience who is mature, responsible and sensitive to a woman's needs, wants more than just sex. An irresponsible, immature, insecure, insensitive c--khound out to prove (1) that he can get it up (2) with anybody he pleases (3) anytime he pleases is preoccupied with self-gratification and really doesn't want more than sex.

And he doesn't deserve more. These men need more than just sex to make them real men but they're too stupid and immature and irresponsible, etc. etc. etc. to know it. These men usually treat women like cannibals treat meat. They chew it up and if they like it, they swallow it. If they don't like it, they spit it out. Regardless of what they do with it, the meat is already a mess just like the lives of many of the women who meet these twentieth-century cannibals who piss and think with the same organ. Give the cannibal a 321 BMW, a polo shirt, a pair of NIKES, a pleather (plastic and leather) briefcase and a slightly exaggerated penis and he thinks he's God's gift to the opposite sex.

60

Even sadder than the cannibal's profile is that a lot of women recognize his M.O. but still proceed to "change" him, to help him find himself. If you feel women have been assigned a job when it comes to men (I never got my instructions), I hope that you at least believe that it's not to change them but to help them believe in someone or something else besides themselves (even if it's not us).

The fact is that if he's lost and he doesn't know he's lost which means he's not looking for *himself* (are you with me?), how in the hell do you think *you* can find him? Eventually he will change but only if he wants to. I know a lot of us have been storing up love for a lot of years but we can't help him if he doesn't make a conscious decision to help himself. And if he's like most cannibals, he probably won't admit he has a problem. If he won't admit it, he can't solve it. If he won't admit it and he can't solve it, how in the hell can you solve it? Frankly, you become the problem because you won't accept him the way he is. "You're the problem" he'll say and he'll be right. Either accept him or move on. Without a real commitment to change, he won't. And that's that.

In all fairness, all of the men we meet are not cannibals. Many are kind and sensitive friends and lovers but unfortunately are haunted by memories of bad childhoods, poor family relationships, ex-wives, ex-girlfriends, rejection, low self-esteem, pursue-conquer-assassinate mentalities, etc.

So what happens? They dump on you. All of their frustrations and guilt trips and boy-man emotions. Immaturity and insecurity seem to be a requirement for this boy-man. He is somewhere between 30 and 50 years old chronologically but behaves like a 13-year old when he's around you. He's selfish, greedy, self-centered and impatient like a teenager who wants the keys to his father's car although he knows that his father has to go to work. And to make matters worse . . . he wants the keys now, this moment!

And the boy-man wants you . . . your heart, your body and your soul if he can get it but only for awhile. Why? He's afraid but ironically, more of himself than of you. Fear has become his best friend and his worst enemy and if you try to separate him from it, you become his next victim. The best thing you can do for him is to ignore him. The best thing you can do for yourself is to stay clear or you'll be eaten alive!

". . . there's no such thing as a free lunch"

CHAPTER 15

THE TRUTH HURTS

I can't deny it. Living solo can be a desperately lonely existence if you allow it to be. It can be filled with fear, anxiety, rejection, herpes, AIDS and single servings of tuna and jello. But wouldn't it be criminal to allow the temporary insecurities that build up because of our singleness make us lose sight of the fact that we deserve a life filled with new experiences and that we have a right to be happy?

In an unending search for Mr. Right—for love, respect, honesty and answers to our loneliness—we must learn to accept the truth. There are simply not enough eligible men to go around. Eliminate the undesirables, add Uncle Toms, scary-curls, pimps, psychopaths and sissies, what have you got? Not a helluva lot!

What then is the answer to our dilemma? Do we continue to search or wait and pray? Do we surrender to our sometimes puritan but always active sexual needs and become "loose women"? Do we allow ourselves to become prey for all of the insecure, egotistical, penis-for-a-brain men who find pleasure in using, manipulating and abusing us? What the hell do we do?

The first step, without a question, is to accept the truth. The unblemished and painful truth is that all of us will not get married. Don't get hysterical. I know the truth hurts but there's more. Some of us may never even fall in love (remember that's a temporary state anyway).

The truth of the matter is that waiting for the perfect man to come into our lives at the perfect time is a perfect waste of time (I made that up. Clever isn't it?) This is not to say we should ever completely give up meeting that "near perfect" mate, but I believe (as you should) that the journey should be as enjoyable as the final destination.

I would like to suggest that if you are a spiritual being, continue to ask God for the mate that he promised all of us. If you are an optimist but not necessarily spiritual, I suggest that you make an honest effort to keep on caring about that occasional "good guy." He may not necessarily be Mr. Right but if he shares the time and space in your life and fills the void in your heart, don't miss a precious moment of it! Remind yourself everyday that nothing in life is certain but change and death. You have choices that only you can make and now is the time to make them.

The next step is to get in touch with your own feelings and your own needs—both emotional and physical. Ask yourself some very serious questions. Do you "need" (not want) a man? Why do you need him? How bad do you need him? How often? What do you want in a man? What will you settle for? Will you settle for less? Can you be happy if you don't find this man? Can you be happy if you don't find *any* man? For how long? Are you strong enough to make a conscious decision to be happy without a man?

These are questions that only you can answer. If you decide to be happy, you will be happy. If you decide to sleepwalk your way through life just because you don't have a man, then so be it. None of us can afford to wait for good things to happen to us. We have to make them happen.

Now for the fun part. Let's do an exercise. Fill out the charts on the following pages. Be honest. (It's your book. You paid for it!). In **EXERCISE I**, don't start with the obvious—physical characteristics like tall or short, thin or fat, etc. or whether or not he has a car or a job. Start with qualities like honesty, patience, kindness, etc. Try to make an honest statement about why these qualities are important to you. In the **COMPROMISE** column, if your answer is "no," explain why. Seeing what you want and what you don't want in black and white gives you an opportunity to not only see a "profile" of the person you want in your life but also allows you to see if you have realistic expectations.

For example, if you want a man who is financially secure (doctor, lawyer, undertaker), it would be unrealistic to dream of meeting someone who stays home everyday and serves you breakfast in bed (when is he supposed to make all of this money?) Again, be honest. Nothing is insignificant if it's important to you. If you are a neat person and need an uncluttered person to share your space, write it down. Sometimes it's the little things that count. Just be sure to write "yes" in the **COMPROMISE** column if it's something that you feel you can sacrifice to acquire something more important.

Now for the hard part. In **EXERCISE II**, you get a free self-analysis. You may think you're a saint but if you're also stubborn, demanding and jealous, write it down. Make a list of personality traits you'd like to work on—

not necessarily to impress someone else—but because you'd feel better about yourself.

Don't try to be paper-perfect (it's a little late, isn't it?) Just try to be as honest as you can about who you are and what you want. There are no perfect answers or perfect people. We live in a society where most people don't run nude down Main Street, urinate in telephone booths or deliberately break wind in public (some people do). So if your answers don't fit the "norm", don't worry about it. In love, there is no norm.

Study both exercises everyday. Feel free to add, delete, rearrange or do whatever it takes to make you feel more comfortable with your assessment of who you are and what you want out of your life. If you learn to be yourself (your best self) and take life exactly the way it's been given to you—abundantly—you won't have to look for happiness. Happiness will come looking for you.

EXERCISE I

WHAT I WANT

WHY?

COMPROMISE?
(If your answer
is no, why not?)

WHAT I DON'T WANT

WHY?

COMPROMISE?
(If your answer
is no, why not?)

EXERCISE II

A FEW GOOD THINGS ABOUT

YOUR NAME

**A FEW THINGS I'D
LIKE TO CHANGE**
(Why?)

A FEW NOT-SO-GOOD THINGS ABOUT

YOUR NAME

**A FEW THINGS I MAY NOT
BE ABLE TO CHANGE**
(Why?)

". . . weeping may endure for a night but joy always comes in the morning"

CHAPTER **16**

BREAKING UP

Let's face it. Some of us get lucky and meet men who can spell the word commitment but even those relationships may (and do) ultimately end in separation. Without a doubt, the end of a relationship can be a devastating experience but only if you allow it.

Women have to learn to let go and remember that the pain will disappear and the wound will heal. Time will cure anything. Expect a few withdrawal pains but redirecting your energy with your family and friends can be the difference between sanity and going over the deep end. We all have an inner reservoir of strength. Look inside yourself and find yours. It will help you get rid of his ghost as soon as possible.

At the same time, examine the relationship very carefully Separate fact from fiction. Ask yourself some very important questions.

Was he your only reason for living? How could he be? You came into this world alone and you're booked on a solo flight home.

Was he the source of your being? How could he be? There are only three things you honestly need to survive on this planet—oxygen, water and food. And since you are the main course in your life, everything else on the menu is gravy. Don't contaminate your body or spirit with anger, hate and fear. Get on your knees and thank God the bastard didn't take your heart and soul with him.

Look at your lost relationship as a stepping stone, not a stumbling block. This will allow you to be alert when you meet a real man—an honest, open man that God has sent your way. If you're walking around in a coma or your vision is clouded by tears, you'll probably miss him.

Surviving the lost relationship should be your primary goal. Losing a lover hurts but it can't kill you. If you can't control your emotions, then you won't have the power to move on. If you don't move on, you'll never get on with your life.

So wipe away your tears, get the lead out of your a-- and kiss that nightmare goodbye!

"...earth's noblest thing—a woman perfected"

CHAPTER **17**

THE FORBIDDEN FRUIT

Black women have a reservoir of love to give and yet we oftentimes ration our love to the very ones who have been denied it for 400 years—Black women.

I LOVE ME! Say it. *I LOVE ME!* Say it like you mean it. *I LOVE ME!* Say it louder. *I LOVE ME!* I do love me and through this love, I have been able to accept my gift of life as a miracle and accept my singleness as another stage in my growth like wearing my first bra (now that was a sight!) or driving a car (I failed the test three times).

I'm still learning to enjoy life as if I were only a heartbeat away from death (aren't we all?) I still suffer from loneliness and unhappiness at times but I am not a lonely and unhappy person. It takes too much time and energy to be depressed all of the time and frankly, I need my energy. I've got things to do, places to go and real people to meet.

Being single can be a problem if you perceive it as a problem. And most people who see it as a problem simply do not love themselves, do not see themselves as lovable and have not taken the time to find out what love is and where it starts—at home. If you are preoccupied with having "a relationship" or obsessed with being married, the bottom line is that you don't love yourself and you may be incapable of loving anyone.

But on the other hand, if you simply want the love, affection and respect of one man at a time (let me repeat that) one man at a time, then perhaps it's time you and I had a serious discussion.

Please don't forget that the problem is bigger than you and I. Watch my lips! How many times have I told you (in this book alone) that there are more single men than single women? I know it takes awhile to sink in (the romantic side of my somewhat undeveloped brain is still fighting the idea).

But what's wrong with being single? Why do most people think there's something wrong with you if you even look like you enjoy being single? In all honesty, it takes a lot of courage and strength to be single and enjoy it, particularly in a society that is preoccupied with love (and sex).

Love sells records, movies, television and toilet paper. If you're single and tired of the salesmen knocking on your brain telling you that you can't be happy without a mate; if you're tired of maintaining a perpetual state of "I-want-to-be-in-love-wedding-day-anticipation-blues," make a commitment today to start enjoying your life. Enjoy yourself, your freedom, your options, your opportunities, your alternatives.

"But what?" you ask "could be an alternative to a life of being alone and manless? Read on.

CHAPTER **18**

ALTERNATIVES

If you really cannot envision yourself without a man and have no desire to live your life to the fullest, here are a few alternatives:

(1) Become a nun: If you want to deal in absolutes, make a beeline to the nearest convent and don't look back.

(2) Become a whore: This is a really sick idea! But if you simply cannot do without a daily dose of sex and prefer men who can't make it with real women, go for it stupid! Can you imagine sleeping with someone who has to pay for a little action?

(3) Date white men (or men from other ethnic groups). We have access to a lot of men today of varying shades but most of us still prefer black men. If you

73

do decide to 'cross over," please make it worth your while. Do it for love or money, not sex. You can date a poor black man. Why would you date a poor yellow or red or white man? Power and money are strong aphrodisiacs and there's a lot of power and money "on the other side." Also, if these men are attracted to you, they are usually as subtle as an octupus. If you are interested, when they start grabbing, grab back!

(4) Date women: If you've made a conscious decision to go on a man-diet and experiment with women, please don't tell me about it. I have no right to sit in judgement but I'm also not as liberal as I sound.

(5) Date undesirables: Please pray for x-ray vision so you can see the truth about these characters. Most of these bums are as intelligent as lint and incapable of giving or accepting love. Unless you are prepared to give 200% and receive less than 10%, leave these psychos alone. Most have severe mental problems, stand on street corners and love to beat women. (Remember Chapter 10?) Their juvenile destructive behavior is a semi-conscious plea for the attention they should have received as children. The best thing this bastard can do for you is to leave you alone. The best thing *you* can do for *you* is leave him alone.

(6) Date a married man: (See Chapter 19 for details)

(7) Become celibate. This is not the worst state to be in (you could have AIDS). Celibacy is a great time to do a little self-examination, re-evaluate your life and set some new goals. It's a great time to find out who you really are and what you really want out of life.

Celibacy is not new (even Cleopatra practiced it occasionally). For centuries, people just like you and me have said "Enough is enough! What is it all for?" Men and women both have refused to become physically involved with a member of the opposite sex just "because." And it has always amazed me how surprised people are when they ask you a personal question about *your* sex life and you tell them you're celibate. But some of the same people who go into shock when you tell them that you're celibate will simply smile when you tell them that you laid the entire defensive line of the Houston Oilers.

Somehow people think that men you desire magically appear when you're sexually excited. They don't. More often than not, they're nowhere to be found. If you prefer making it with someone just to keep in practice, I really think you have a problem. If you prefer battle scars that rarely heal from undesirables over celibacy and peace of mind, I'd seek professional help! And if you think you're the only person in the world (man or woman) practicing celibacy, think again.

(8) The only other alternative you have is to kill yourself but don't be a fool, fool!

"... love without hope is nothing"

CHAPTER **19**

THE NO-ALTERNATIVE
ALTERNATIVE
(BECOMING THE OTHER WOMAN)

I devoted an entire chapter to this masochistic, self-defeating alternative (I call it "bootleg love") because as we get older, many of us begin to see married men as a solution to the "I'm-still-not-married-syndrome."

I dare you to deny that you have not said or heard at least 100 times in the last week "All of the good ones are married!" A lot of us don't personally agree with this revelation but nevertheless, we nod our heads and perpetuate the myth to justify our lack of companionship. After all, as beautiful and intelligent and successful as we are, what other reason could there be for our singleness? Bullsh-t!

Number 1: All of the good ones are not married. In fact, a lot of the ones who are married are not only bad for their wives, they'd be worse for you. A married man who "fools" around (take a hint, fool!) has already made a definite statement about his character. He's already proven he's a liar, a cheat and a thief (he's stealing precious moments from his wife and the best years of your life). He's also dishonest, selfish, egotistical and most of all, untrustworthy. The list goes on and on and on.

I personally believe that I have too much love to give to someone who can love me genuinely and openly than to give it to this greedy S.O.B.! After all, what can he offer me? A few stolen moments, in and out of my life (and my bed) twice a week? No birthdays, holidays or vacations-for-two? No warm body to snuggle next to past dawn on a cold and rainy Sunday morning? No shoulder to cry on late at night after the crazies on your job have made you crazy?

What can he offer me? An occasional telephone call, an occasional screw and a lot of heartaches. Why take the risk? You can get the call, the screw and a lot less heartaches for half the risk.

"But there are no single men," you say. I beg to differ. You may not know a lot of single men or even like the ones you know but that doesn't mean that they aren't out there. We're out there and they're out there. There may be fewer of them and we may pass like ships in the night but I truly believe that there are men—real men—who are looking for something besides a quickie.

But that is not the point. The point is whether or not you believe that something is better than nothing even if (1) it doesn't belong to you and (2) it's not what you want. And let's not forget that the entire situation is complicated by the fact that you're not what **he** wants either. If he wanted you, he'd wake up in **your** bed every morning and not his wife's. Think about it.

Number 2: According to a recent survey, 72% of married men have been unfaithful at one time or another in their marriage. Why should you become another statistic, particularly since the study went on to point out that the majority of these men *do not*—let me repeat that—*do not* divorce their wives to marry "the other woman." In fact, many of them probably have multiple relationships of which you are simply one.

I realize that none of us are immune to pain in a relationship but why allow some selfish, egotistical, lying, married jackass to hurt you when a single guy can serve the same purpose without the baggage (his wife?) In fact thinking about a married man who cheats on his wife should make you angry.

Get angry. Get real angry. How dare he think he can have the best of both worlds—a loving wife and a wifely lover? How dare he think he deserves all of the love and tenderness and compassion and fire that you've been saving up for all of these years to give to someone who can return it openly and honestly?

These men always want more than they can and will give. The odds are against you from the very beginning. His lies will reach epidemic proportions about everything from why he can't see you one night to whether or not he still screws his wife (although she's three months pregnant). What kind of promises can he make you? How many will he have to break because of his "extenuating circumstances?" How long can you accept his broken promises? Why should you?

Becoming the other woman can never be a real alternative for a woman who loves herself and who knows that the price you have to pay is too high. If you crave uncertainty and your i.q. is less than your age, go for it. But you should never want to become *a* woman in your man's life but *the* woman in his life!

". . . it's not what you call me but what I answer to"

CHAPTER **20**

BUT I WANT CHILDREN!

So you're single and you want children? As long as you select their father with care, don't have them by a married man and can afford to take care of them, have children. It's your decision . . . your body . . . your life.

"But what will people think?"

Screw people! Unless they're paying your house note, car note and American Express *in full each month*, screw 'em! God is the only one you have to answer to and he's the only one who doesn't ask questions. He already knows the answers.

Now stop asking stupid questions and finish the last chapter!

". . . you wouldn't have to count the days if you made each day count"

CHAPTER **21**

THE SIMS SOLUTION

This is—without question—the most important chapter in this book. It is based on the fact—not assumption—that every available single woman is not going to get married, some of us may never be blessed with an exclusive long-term relationship and even if we wander into a "real" relationship, it may not lead us to matrimony.

But none of these facts give us a license to magnify the problem, ignore our alternatives and sink into a deep depression because of the void in our lives. Frankly, it was because of this void in my own life that I was inspired by God to write this book. I am here to tell you that you don't have to feel powerless anymore. You don't have to dwell on the fact that life isn't fair (who said it would be?). You don't have to consider suicide 24-hours a day. All you have to do is change your attitude about being single.

Today's single Black woman is just another test of black womanhood—of our endurance and strength. It is also a testimony to countless other black women whose problems far surpassed that of being alone. Problems like how to keep your baby from being sold the moment he was born; how to stay on your feet in a cottonfield when it's 90 degrees and you're eight months pregnant; how to make your man feel like a man for a few hours every night when he's been on his knees for fourteen hours. And most importantly, how to stay alive.

If there is a single thread that holds all black people together, it is endurance dipped in faith and polished with hope. Black women wrote the book on endurance. We are the original victors but we've had our share of experiences as victims.

We've been victims of racism and watched as our men were stripped of their self-respect and pride.

We've been victims of the Vietnam War that robbed us of the cream-of-the-crop of our brave black men.

We've been victims of the violence and turmoil of the sixties that robbed us of men of character and strength and vision.

We're still victims of poverty, pimps, prostitution, drug addicts, alcoholism, homosexuality, pseudo-sophisticated three-piece-suit-wearing professional Uncle Toms and of course, Mr. Charlies with misplaced values.

We're victims of our own men who—because they control so little in America—try to control us through fear, insecurity, false pride and pain. And although all of us are concerned about the plight of Black people in this country, black chauvanism is alive and living in this sexist, racist society.

But even as victims, we cannot afford the luxury of acting like victims. Black women have never been *totally* dependent on our men for anything. We've not had that luxury. So waiting for Mr. Right to come and take us away "from all of this" is just not consistent with reality. Some of us are robbing ourselves of the best years of our lives because we are putting all of our energies into finding that "perfect" mate. The evidence of our consuming desire for Mr. Right hangs over most of us like a shadow. We write off all potentially decent, temporary relationships and hold out for that mystical, long-term permanent relationship that oftentimes is just that—a mystery.

But everything in our lives is temporary. Rather than buy a home, you choose to live in a 500-square foot apartment because "a house is something my husband and I will select together." You don't have a husband (or a boyfriend sometimes) so you don't take vacations because *everybody* knows that "single women can't take vacations alone!" And if you find a boyfriend and you've already been there, where would you go? And don't forget the diamond ring. You'd like one but everybody knows that "women don't buy themselves diamonds." That's bull-sh-t and you know it but the list goes on and on and on.

So at 35 or 40, most of us will look back on our lives and wonder how we allowed ourselves to have so many unlived experiences—like buying a home, traveling to the Caribbean, buying that "genuine diamond ring" or expensive fur coat. But even beyond those unlived experiences, it is the unfulfilled human potential that is most damaging.

We are so busy preparing for the future with someone else that we never fully develop the person who has always been our best and truest friend and companion—ourselves. We are our greatest personal asset but we will never be able to see the beauty of our own world if we refuse to be responsible for our own happiness. I refuse to explain or apologize for being single. Not when I have unlimited opportunities to learn new skills, to develop new talents, meet new friends and make new discoveries every day of my life.

Women have shown throughout history that we have unlimited potential despite hundreds of years of racist, sexist attitudes and now we have unlimited opportunities and choices to match our potential. For years, we have been content to settle for less—less money for our labor, less credit for our contributions, less sex for our needs, less love than we deserve. In short, we have not only had to fight off the chains of racism but the shackles of second class citizenship because we (through no fault of our own) were born women.

Most of us are in the twilight zone—somewhere between here and now and there and nowhere. We cannot continue to sleepwalk through single life or imitate human beings or wait for an unreliable "prop" that we believe can breathe life into our lifeless bodies.

The principal business of life is to enjoy it and enjoy it while we have it—here and now. Each of us has to take the responsibility for our own happiness, our own peace of mind and our own contentment. But what is contentment? Contentment is not assuming a defeatist attitude or giving up ever finding that "perfect" (or near perfect) mate for you. Contentment is a realistic awareness that with or without a man, you will survive (unless you are stupid enough to kill yourself!). How—and not if—you survive then becomes the question.

And since it is your life, it becomes your question. You can choose to sit idly by and watch your twenties, thirties and forties slip by (most men never feel they slip by gracefully for women) or you can take charge of your life today and make it an unforgettable experience, a happening today and everyday. And even if you don't find what you're looking for, by living each day to the fullest, you may find something greater—greater contentment, greater happiness, greater rewards.

Changing things on the outside won't help unless you're ready to change on the inside. We have to change our attitude—about men, about sex, about being alone. Somehow we have become our greatest enemies. Somehow we have allowed ourselves to become victims of the past and crippled ourselves in the process. Today, even we have a problem seeing the issue clearly so how do we expect our men to understand our feelings, our frustrations, our fears?

The issue is not whether or not being married or single is right or wrong. The issue is not whether or not we—as single Black women—want to be single. Many of us don't. The issue is whether or not we can adjust to being single for the rest of our lives if we have to.

I think we can. I believe we can turn this so-called-male shortage into an opportunity to learn to love ourselves again, to develop our God-given talents, to appreciate the things we have started taking for granted—good health, good friends, parents, a decent job, a nice house, a car that runs, whatever.

We must learn to say "thank you" for the qualities that make life worth living—love, joy, peace and for the wisdom to know that we must change because change is inevitable. We must learn that our being single gives us a chance to become more mature—accepting life the way it is but knowing that it too will change with time.

We have to learn to love ourselves so much that with or without a mate, we still know that we are loved. And remember, if you love yourself, you will never feel unloved.

So, please don't weep for me! I am loved. My mother loves me, God loves me and more importantly, I love myself. I'm alive, I'm healthy and my life is unfolding just the way it should. And whether you choose to believe it or not, your life is unfolding just the way it should. You're alive (if you're reading this book), you're healthy (I hope so) and somebody, somewhere loves you (I know God does!).

With all of the good things you've got going for yourself, how can you be concerned because you're missing one slice from the pie of life—a man? The rest of the pie is yours for the asking and all you have to do is make a decision to grab it and run. It's your life . . . so *live* it . . . with or without a man!